LIBRARY
COMMUNITY HIGH SCHOOL
326 Joliet St.
West Chicago, ILL. 60185

DEMCO

FOCUS ON
FAMILY
MATTERS

Understanding
Post-Traumatic
Stress Disorder

FOCUS ON FAMILY MATTERS

Focus on Family Matters

Understanding Post-Traumatic Stress Disorder

Marvin Rosen, Ph.D.

CHELSEA HOUSE
PUBLISHERS
A Haights Cross Communications Company
Philadelphia

CHELSEA HOUSE PUBLISHERS

EDITOR IN CHIEF Sally Cheney
DIRECTOR OF PRODUCTION Kim Shinners
CREATIVE MANAGER Takeshi Takahashi
MANUFACTURING MANAGER Diann Grasse

Staff for UNDERSTANDING POST-TRAUMATIC STRESS DISORDER

ASSOCIATE EDITOR Bill Conn
PICTURE RESEARCHER Sarah Bloom
PRODUCTION ASSISTANT Jaimie Winkler
COVER AND SERIES DESIGNER Takeshi Takahashi
LAYOUT 21st Century Publishing and Communications, Inc.

A Haights Cross Communications Company

http://www.chelseahouse.com

First Printing

1 3 5 7 9 8 6 4 2

Library of Congress Cataloging-in-Publication Data
Rosen, Marvin.
  Understanding post-traumatic stress disorder / Marvin Rosen.
     p. cm. — (Focus on family matters)
Summary: A discussion of the pyschological disorder known as Post Traumatic Stress Disorder, how it affects young people, and what can be done to treat this condition. Includes bibliographical references and index.
  ISBN 0-7910-6951-6
 1. Post-traumatic stress disorder—Juvenile literature. [1.
Post-traumatic stress disorder.] I. Title. II. Series.
  RC552.P67 R6674 2002
  616.85'21—dc21

                          2002006504

Contents

Introduction

Marvin Rosen, Ph.D.
Consulting Editor

B ad things sometimes happen to good people. We've probably all heard that expression. But what happens when the "good people" are teenagers?

Growing up is stressful and difficult to negotiate. Teenagers are struggling to becoming independent, trying to cut ties with their families that they see as restrictive, burdensome, and unfair. Rather than attempting to connect in new ways with their parents, they may withdraw. When bad things do happen, this separation may make the teen feel alone in coping with difficult and stressful issues.

Focus on Family Matters provides teens with practical information about how to cope when bad things happen to them. The series deals foremost with feelings—the emotional pain associated with adversity. Grieving, fear, anger, stress, guilt, and sadness are addressed head on. Teens will gain valuable insight and advice about dealing with their feelings, and for seeking help when they cannot help themselves.

The authors in this series identify some of the more serious problems teens face. In so doing, they make three assumptions: First, teens who find themselves in difficult situations are not at fault and should not blame themselves. Second, teens can overcome difficult situations, but may need help to do so. Third, teens bond with their families, and the strength of this bond influences their ability to handle difficult situations.

These books are also about communication—specifically about the value of communication. None of the problems covered occurs in a vacuum, and none of the situations should be faced by anyone alone. Each either involves a close family member or affects the entire family. Since families teach teens how to trust, relate to others, and solve problems, teens need to bond with families to develop normally and become emotionally whole. Success in dealing with adversity depends not only on the strength of the individual teen, but also upon the resources of the family in providing support, advice, and material assistance. Strong attachment to care givers in a supporting, nurturing, safe family structure is essential to successful coping.

Some teens learn to cope with adversity—they absorb the pain, they adjust, and they go on. But for others, the trauma they experience seems like an insurmountable challenge—they become angry, stressed, and depressed. They may withdraw from friends, they may stop going to school, and their grades may slip. They may draw negative attention to themselves and express their pain and fear by rebelling. Yet, in each case, healing can occur.

The teens who cope well with adversity, who are able to put the past behind them and regain their momentum, are no less sensitive or caring than those who suffer most. Yet there is a difference. Teens who are more resilient to trauma are able to dig deep down into their own resources, to find strength in their families and in their own skills, accomplishments, goals, aspirations, and values. They are able to find reasons for optimism and to feel confidence in their capabilities. This series recognizes the effectiveness of these strategies, and presents problem-solving skills that every teen can use.

Focus on Family Matters is positive, optimistic, and supportive. It gives teens hope and reinforces the power of their own efforts to handle adversity. And most importantly, it shows teens that while they cannot undo the bad things that have happen, they have the power to shape their own futures and flourish as healthy, productive adults.

What is Post-Traumatic Stress Disorder?

■ Maria is lucky to be alive. When she was three years old, she fell into a well in her family's backyard. She had been playing in the soggy grass near the covered opening when suddenly the ground gave way. She fell a long way down, finally becoming wedged in a narrow space. She called and called to her mother before she was located. It took firemen and rescue workers nearly 36 hours before they could pull her out to safety. Now, nine years later, Maria dreams nearly every night about that horrible experience, waiting in the deep, dark hole. She can still smell the damp, musty smell of the ground. She can still feel the way she felt all those years ago— trapped, her legs not able to move. They say she is lucky, and that her rescue was a miracle, but Maria isn't so sure. She struggles through that long, terrible experience, reliving it nearly every night.

All of us have experienced a time when we felt frightened. You may have felt anxious about a test, worried about a competition, tense at the prospect of an argument with your parents.

Post-traumatic stress disorder (PTSD) occurs when the emotional effects of a horrible or frightening experience are felt long after the event has passed. The event may be a personal one—like a car accident—or one that affects many people—like the bombings of the World Trade Center on September 11, 2001.

But **post-traumatic stress disorder** (or PTSD) is something quite different from these ordinary, common fears. If you suffer from PTSD, the fear almost never disappears. It is a constant reminder of a specific, horrible event—a **trauma**—that you or someone you know experienced.

PTSD was first diagnosed in soldiers at the beginning of

the 20th century. American troops that had fought in horrible, bloody battles in World War I returned to the U.S. complaining of unusual symptoms. Their muscles would quiver, or their bodies would shake, but the shaking was not related to any specific, physical problem. Finally, doctors correctly determined that the shaking and other

How does PTSD

differ from normal feelings of anxiety and nervousness?

symptoms were related to the terrible events the soldiers had witnessed in battle. It was described as "battle fatigue" or "war neurosis," terms that did not fully explain how severe the suffering was or how long-term its effects could be without proper treatment.

Today, psychiatrists use the term post-traumatic stress disorder to describe this condition. The symptoms may be somewhat different, but the suffering is the same. When you experience an overwhelmingly frightening event—one in which it seems possible that you could die or be seriously injured—PTSD is often the result. This event may be something you experience directly, or it may be something you see happening to someone else. You may even suffer from PTSD if a family member or close friend suffers a traumatic event and then shares the experience with you.

Whatever the event, and whether it has happened to you or to someone you care about, your reaction will be the same: disbelief, intense fear, even horror. When you suffer from PTSD, you feel helpless. You may find it difficult to sit still for any long period of time. You may find it difficult to keep track of homework assignments or impossible to organize a report. If you suffer from PTSD, you will find it difficult to function in school or at home, and you will continue to re-live the horrible experience, long after it happened.

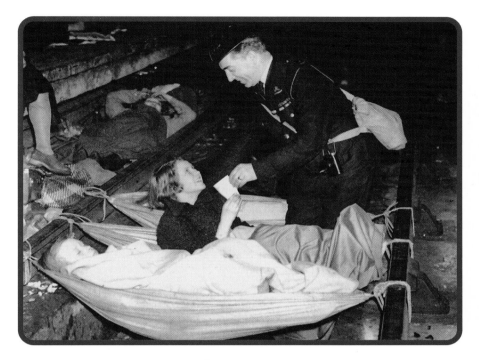

First identified in soldiers, PTSD was found to affect not only combat troops, but also civilians who experienced or witnessed traumatic events. Repeated air raids on London during World War II produced PTSD in many British civilians.

How does it happen?

A wide variety of extreme experiences can produce PTSD. As we discussed earlier, PTSD was first diagnosed in soldiers. It often results from war experiences on the battle-field or during an air raid or invasion. (British citizens who lived through the bombing of London in World War II commonly experienced PTSD after the war had ended.) PTSD may follow a personal assault, such as a robbery, hijacking, rape, physical or sexual abuse, terrorist attack, earthquake or automobile accident. PTSD can happen after witnessing or learning about the sudden, unexpected death of a loved one. The closer to, and more involved you are, with a traumatic event, the more intense your reaction will be.

Traditionally, psychiatrists believed that PTSD was caused by a single, terrible event. Increasingly, however, mental health professionals have grown to recognize that another category of trauma can also result in symptoms of PTSD. When a patient has a history of continued threat of physical or sexual abuse, or exposure to violence, all of the symptoms of PTSD can also occur. In fact, PTSD often results when you believe that the frightening experience was not a single, isolated event but instead could occur again.

What is PTSD?

While PTSD can occur following a wide range of experiences, and while its symptoms may be quite varied, there are three characteristic features of PTSD. The first is that you may continue to re-live the trauma—continue to think about it, to feel it and to worry about each detail—long after it actually took place. Second, you will avoid any situation that is similar to or reminds you of the original experience. Third, you will be constantly watching and waiting for a repeat of the experience, and feeling very anxious.

How would it feel to relive a traumatic event over and over again?

There are many ways in which you might re-live the frightening event. It is as if the experience is constantly popping into your thoughts. All of the painful emotions that you originally felt are experienced again. This may happen in the form of a nightmare that comes night after night.

In rare cases, some people even have **flashbacks**— reliving the experience as if in a dream, even though they

Following a traumatic event, you may continue to re-live the experience in dreams or while awake. Fear of similar experiences may affect your ability to sleep, concentrate, or study in school. These effects are all part of PTSD.

are awake. Their eyes may be open, but they react as if they are dreaming, reliving the experience as if it was actually happening again. They do not realize that it is not really happening. There is a scientific term for this process of being unable to separate what is happening now from the horrible experience that happened some time ago—it is called being in a **dissociative state**. It can last just a few seconds to several hours and even several days. It may be triggered by anything reminding the person of the original trauma, such as the anniversary of the event, and usually is extremely painful for the person suffering through it.

It is common to try to avoid any circumstance, experience, or place associated with the horrible event. You may try not to think or talk about it; you may avoid activities or situations that are related to that event. As a result, you may become deliberately unable to remember anything about the experience. But your body responds to this "forced forgetfulness" with other symptoms. You may feel numb, exhausted, empty. You may find it difficult to feel at all. It is as if by blocking out the strong emotions surrounding the terrible event, you manage to block out all feelings altogether. Needless to say, this emptiness and inability to feel makes it quite difficult to enjoy your life, to keep up friendships, to interact with other people.

Some PTSD sufferers may be unable to forget what happened. They may constantly feel anxious. They have trouble falling asleep at night. They may find it impossible to concentrate at school. They seem always to be looking over their shoulder, expecting something bad to happen. They may be extremely sensitive, misinterpreting or misunderstanding harmless words or innocent actions. They may be

What would you do

if you thought you were suffering from PTSD?

irritable with frequent outbursts of anger. They startle easily. They may feel that they are damaged and will never lead a normal life.

In some instances PTSD can be followed by even more

serious psychiatric disorders, such as depression, panic disorder, obsessive-compulsive behavior, specific phobias or fears, or substance abuse.

How often does this occur?

It is difficult to estimate how often PTSD occurs. Different studies have provided different estimates of how many people suffer from PTSD. Clearly, in times of war or disaster such as the attack on the World Trade Center, more people will experience PTSD—depending on how many people were affected by the disaster, and how close they were to the actual event. We are, in some ways, the victims of modern communications and advanced technology. As more and more people have access to cell phones, e-mail, and the Internet, as the scope of television coverage has increased to include dramatic footage from disaster scenes, wars and terrorist attacks, more of us will experience traumatic events almost as if we were there, in the midst of the crisis. And many more people will suffer PTSD.

How long does it last?

PTSD can occur at any age. It usually begins within the first three months after the event. But can also happen for the first time months, or even years, later. In over half the cases the symptoms may disappear within three months. In other instances PTSD may last for years.

How likely are you to develop PTSD? Many factors make a difference in why people develop PTSD. These include your personality, your early childhood experiences, your family history, and the emotional support available to you from family and friends. These factors are covered in more detail in Chapter 3.

The Big Picture: Anxiety and Anxiety Disorders

John hates to get into a car. He walks or bikes whenever he can. He feels panicked simply knowing he will have to drive somewhere— anywhere. One moment in an ordinary day changed his life. His father had driven him to a dentist appointment, parking on the fifth level of a parking garage near the dentist's office. When the appointment was over, they got into the car to drive home. John's father, distracted by a problem at work, thought that he was backing the car up, but instead put it in drive. He stepped on the gas, and the car lurched forward, breaking through the restraining barriers of the parking garage. For two hours, John and his father sat in that car as it dangled five stories above the street. They were afraid to move, afraid to speak, for fear that the car, balancing on the edge, would tip over and fall to the ground. Finally, a tow truck pulled the car back into the garage, but John relives the fear of that experience every time he gets into a car. His friends talk about getting their drivers' licenses in two more years. John can't imagine ever looking forward to getting into a car again.

PTSD is only one of a number of anxiety disorders. These disorders occur when our normal response to danger gets out of control and begins to affect our daily lives—even when no danger exists.

There are many common names for the condition psychologists refer to as anxiety. You may call it tension, or nerves, or stress, or pressure. You may say that you feel jittery or shaky. It feels like something bad is going to happen. You may feel afraid of something, but not sure what it is that is frightening you. When anxiety gets out of hand, when it causes physical or psychological symptoms such as PTSD, it is referred to as an **anxiety disorder**.

Anxiety is more than just an unpleasant feeling. It is a group of bodily changes and it involves certain behaviors. It is a process that is built into our nervous systems and it has a purpose.

A little biology

An animal in the wild needs a wide range of biological resources—physical skills and responses—to help it survive many different emergencies. These skills and responses are called **survival mechanisms**. A small animal, such as a rabbit, must be able to survive being chased by a predator, like a fox. When the rabbit spots the fox, it needs the right response— usually to run away! Nature has given the rabbit certain abilities to help it cope with life in the wild. For example, when the rabbit sees a fox or other predator, its adrenal glad will give off a chemical (called epinephron) that triggers certain reactions. The rabbit's heart beats faster. Blood rushes to its muscles and brain. It breathes more quickly. These and other changes prepare the rabbit's body for quick reaction and rapid movement. In other animals, similar survival mechanisms will make it possible for it to fight off predators. Biologists call this the **fight or flight mechanism** —the body's ability to survive by choosing either fight (battling a predator) or flight (running away).

Can you describe

how the fight or flight mechanism might help you in an emergency?

Humans also have these mechanisms to help deal with a dangerous situation. In some people, the fight or flight mechanism works overtime. It doesn't shut off, even when there is no crisis. This is when we experience anxiety. When the survival mechanism doesn't switch back off, even after the crisis is over, the feelings of anxiety stay with us. The survival mechanism is no longer helping us to survive—it is interfering with our ability to lead our daily lives.

A little psychology

Psychologists have been thinking about and studying the link between physical responses like survival mechanisms and emotional responses like feelings for more than a century. One theory—from the psychologist and philosopher William James—was that the emotions we feel are merely our awareness of the body's reactions. For example, a man goes into the forest, sees a bear, and runs away. Most of us would explain that the man saw the bear, became afraid, and ran. William James disagreed. He believed that the man saw the bear, ran away, became aware that he was running, and then felt afraid.

Today we understand that the brain plays an important role in our emotions and feelings. We see the bear. We have learned that bears are dangerous. Our body reacts. We tell ourselves that we might be killed and we run. Research has demonstrated that both physical and emotional processes are involved. Memories, things we have learned, and cues

What roles do physical and emotional responses play in creating feelings?

from that particular situation all contribute to the specific feeling or emotion we have in different circumstances.

Anxiety can hurt

Anxiety not only affects your mind; it can affect your body as well. There are many illnesses and conditions—things like ulcers, asthma, hives and headaches—that are caused by or made worse by anxiety. High levels of anxiety can even cause hypertension (high blood

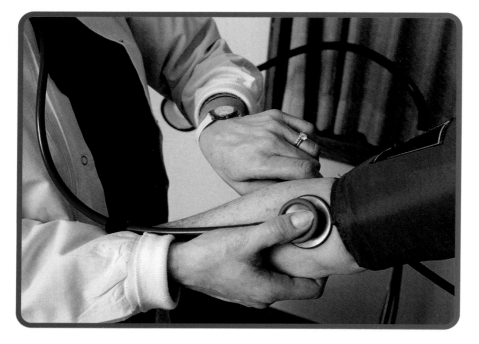

Chronic anxiety can affect our health. People with PTSD and other anxiety disorders often develop stomach ulcers, sleep disorders, and high blood pressure.

pressure), leading to heart disease. There is even evidence that shows that anxiety can suppress your immune system, making you more likely to develop infections and even diabetes or cancer.

The same crisis does not always cause the same levels of anxiety in different people. Some people appear to be more resistant to anxiety, while others seem to be much more likely to develop it.

We use the term **stressors** to refer to influences or factors that may cause anxiety in people. Of course these are different for each person. They include such things as life changes (moving, for example), family changes (such as divorce), financial problems, school pressure, or the death of a loved one. The more of these stressors that you experience at any one time, the more likely it is that you will develop anxiety.

There are many different conditions that spark anxiety. A conflict—being torn in two directions—may make you anxious. Perhaps you are good at music and enjoy playing the drums. But you also love to play soccer. Soccer practice and band practice are both at the same time after school. Friends from the band are pressuring you to join them, but the soccer coach has told you that you are a talented athlete and can make a valuable contribution to the team. What do you do? The choice seems to force you not only to make a decision about how you want to spend your afternoons but what talents matter most to you and even who your friends will be. The result: anxiety. The anxiety will linger until a choice is made.

Conflict can also happen when a choice has pros and cons. Perhaps choosing to play in the band means a year-long commitment to play at football and basketball games and to travel to band competitions. Maybe soccer practices start in the summer, before the school year, and limit your opportunities to take a summer job or family vacation.

We all learn to think and behave in certain ways to reduce our anxiety. We call these mechanisms **defenses**. For example, Joe controls anxiety by becoming a perfectionist, by doing his homework the second he gets home from school, by making sure that all of his chores are done right away, and by always trying to be accurate, neat, and right. If, for some reason, something interferes with these behaviors, Joe feels anxious. Perhaps, after staying up all night completing a term paper, he forgets to bring it to school and misses the deadline. Joe may be in trouble with his teacher but he is in worse trouble with himself.

One mechanism that some people develop is the need to feel in control of any situation. If your group of friends is making plans, you want to be the one to decide where you will go and what you will do. You want to decide who will or won't be invited to a party. You not only want to be the leader—you *need* to be the leader, no matter what the circumstances.

An interesting experiment performed with rats shows how important control can be. In the experiment, there were two sets of rats. All rats received electric shocks, but the first group of rats was given the ability to turn off the shocks. The other group could not. The experiment was, believe it or not, designed to study the formation of ulcers. And which group of rats developed ulcers? The rats that could not turn off the shock. Clearly, the ability to control a frightening and potentially painful situation—or more important, the *lack* of control—made a key difference in the health of the rats.

The lesson for humans is obvious—we can deal with stressful situations better when we have some kind of control over them. Similar experiments have shown that we can better handle shocks and stressful situations if we have some advance warning that they are coming. Random, sudden and unexpected crises are the most difficult to handle, and generally have longer-term effects.

Can you describe some of the defense mechanisms you use to control anxiety?

Family support is another critical factor in determining how we survive a crisis, and how anxious we ultimately become after it. The traditional Japanese culture emphasizes the importance of strong family ties. Older people are honored and often live with their married children. To show how strong family support can affect health, a study of the frequency of heart attacks was done with three groups of

Japanese families. The first group lived in Japan, the second in Hawaii, and the third in California. The study showed that the fewest heart attacks occurred in Japan, while slightly more occurred in families in Hawaii. The most occurred in California, where Japanese-Americans had developed more "American" family structures, with married children living apart from their parents and older adults often living alone.

Finally, how and why we experience anxiety can be determined by our personality. There are many different labels for different personality "types." Some people are described as "Type A"—they are ambitious, hardworking, and often very focused on their goals. "Type B" personalities are more relaxed, fun-loving and less worried about success or the future. Which personality type do you think normally suffers more stress-related illnesses? The Type A personality, of course.

Anxiety disorders

There are many different conditions that psychiatrists describe as anxiety disorders. In addition to PTSD, these include generalized (not specific) anxiety, specific **phobias** or fears, obsessive compulsive disorder, and panic attacks. The common element in all of these different conditions is the constant and excessive feeling of fear, anxiety, worry, and dread. What is the difference between "normal" worry and a medial diagnosis of something like generalized anxiety? Psychiatrists use the description "generalized anxiety" for a condition that has lasted at least six months.

Phobias, or fears, are generally very specific—a fear of heights, for example, or of spiders, or of small or closed places (like an elevator or tunnel). In agoraphobia, people are afraid of places from which it might be difficult to escape. In obsessive compulsive disorders, people suffer

Fears aren't always related to events. Sometimes specific things, like spiders, can provoke a strong fear response. Other common fears, also called phobias, include a fear of heights and fear of enclosed spaces.

from constantly repeated thoughts or worries (obsessions) or rituals (compulsions) or both. A person might be obsessed with a fear of germs, and so feel the need to spend a lot of time washing his hands. This is a way of handling anxiety.

Panic disorder is yet another type of anxiety. A person who suffers from this may honestly believe that they are dying, or going crazy, or having a heart attack. They will feel overwhelmed by terror, and even may find themselves gasping for breath or feel some kind of chest pain.

> **What is an anxiety disorder**
>
> **and how does it differ from normal feelings of anxiety?**

PTSD has certain points in common with these other anxiety disorders. People suffering from PTSD continue to suffer the traumatic experience over and over again. They feel real and vivid physical reactions to their anxiety, in addition to their emotional reactions. And they will go to great lengths to avoid anything that reminds them of the traumatic experience.

Why are they acting this way?

One last explanation may also clarify PTSD. Most of the time, our personalities seem whole, consistent, and predictable. When you know someone well, you have an idea of how they will behave in different situations, and usually they do.

But when people suffer from PTSD, they begin to act in unexpected ways. They may behave in a way that is not consistent with their usual personality. In some cases, they may not seem to remember the original trauma.

Psychiatrists believe that this may happen when the memories of the horrible event have been pushed back as a defense against the anxiety that those memories spark. But the memories are not completely erased—they come back in nightmares or flashbacks.

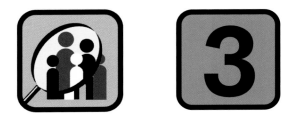

Why Me?

■ Sandy was sexually abused by her father when she was four years old. He had been touching her inappropriately in the bathtub. She knew something was wrong, but she had learned to trust her parents. Finally, she talked about it with her mother. Her father left their home and she has never seen him again. She is now 13, but she has never forgotten it. It bothered her that her father never went to prison for what he did. She was very angry about this. Because of these feelings, she was referred to a support group for teen-aged girls who all had been sexually abused as children. Shortly after beginning these group meetings, Sandy began to have strange experiences. For a few minutes, she seemed to tune out what was going on around her. It seemed that her father was in the room with her and that he was coming after her with a knife. These episodes occurred in school as well as at home. Once it happened in a psychologist's office after she had been referred for psychotherapy. The psychologist believed that the support group experience was upsetting Sandy. Other girls were describing their abuse experiences and Sandy was also expected to

We can't control or predict the horrible events that often cause PTSD. We don't make them happen, and the disorder isn't our fault. What we can do is to try and understand and treat the symptoms of post-traumatic stress.

reveal her abuse. Sandy stopped going to the group meetings and the flashbacks stopped. This did not cure her PTSD, but she was not ready to talk about what had happened with other girls her own age. She needed to sort it out, to process it, first with the help of a trained professional. With the help of a psychologist, Sandy began to make real progress.

In this chapter we will talk about the reasons why you have symptoms of PTSD. We cannot, of course, explain why the trauma itself happened. Sometimes there is no reason, no excuse for a horrible event, much as we may want there to be some explanation. Bad things happen, often to good people. You didn't make it happen. You couldn't control it or predict it. But what you *can* do is begin to understand the symptoms of PTSD, and why you may have developed fears and flashbacks and nightmares when others at the scene did not.

As you learned in the last chapter, PTSD may occur after exposure to a variety of intense and frightening circumstances. Yet not everyone responds in the same way. Some people develop all of the symptoms described earlier, while others seem to be able to resist the distressing and often devastating effects of the trauma. It may be that the first group is more vulnerable to stress reactions while the second has resistance. Let's talk about why these differences exist.

Big and little trauma

First, it is obvious that the characteristics of the trauma itself will influence how intense your reaction will be. It makes a difference if you are exposed to violence up close, or at a distance. Perhaps it is something that is in the news or on TV, such as a terrorist attack. It may have happened to a close relative or friend. It may have involved a limited number of people—such as an airline crash—or thousands.

It matters if it seems likely that the events will occur again. Your age matters, too. Young children worry most about their own safety. As you get older, you learn to worry about those close to you, as well. Your family represents a source of security and support.

Social and political conditions are also important. Conditions of war, terrorism, racial violence, poverty, and political uncertainty all serve to increase feelings of anxiety and to increase risk for PTSD.

> **Can you name** some of the factors that may increase your risk for developing PTSD?

Another important factor is the number of times you have been exposed to trauma. While the cause of PTSD was at one time thought to be related to a single traumatic experience, such as a natural disaster, increasingly experts are becoming aware that PTSD sufferers have had a history of multiple or repeated exposure to trauma. One source of repeated exposure may be in the form of repeated reminders of what happened. PTSD sufferers frequently experience symptoms on the anniversary of the original experience.

How you make a difference

More important than the factors we've discussed at the beginning of this chapter is your belief or perception that the danger continues. This depends upon you—what kind of trauma you've suffered before, how you cope with stress, whether or not you expect to receive outside help and support, and how well you generally cope with life and how good your problem-solving skills are. A person who develops PTSD feels helpless and unable to protect himself from danger. If you have a reasonable expectation that the trauma may occur again—for example, if your family is abusive or you live in a violent community—you will have a much greater chance of developing the symptoms of PTSD.

Coping effectively with PTSD is easier with the help and support of people close to us. Family and friends can help us talk about our feelings and conquer our fears. You may be able to help someone get over their anxiety by listening to them.

It should be apparent that this process is complex. But one thing seems clear. You are better able to handle a traumatic event or experience if you have supportive family members and friends. If you are reading this book because you know someone—a friend or family member—who you think might be suffering from PTSD, remember that you can play a critical role in helping them. Your reactions—your ability to move past the horrible experience and go on with your life—will help others do the same. Your willingness to discuss the experience with them, but also to continue to focus on the future, will prove

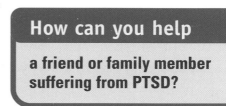

How can you help

a friend or family member suffering from PTSD?

helpful in their efforts to cope. Without this kind of support and care, they may lose hope, seeing only the possibility of negative consequences. They may develop other coping mechanisms, trying to distance themselves physically or emotionally from danger or even forgetting that it occurred.

Secondary factors

Sometimes a war or other disaster has additional, secondary effects that contribute to or emphasize the symptoms of PTSD. Ordinary life may be disrupted. There may not be enough to eat or drink; there may be illness or malnutrition. Schooling may be interrupted. Families may be separated or may come apart. Family members may be lost. You may be forced to leave your home.

When London was bombed during World War II, children were sent to the homes of strangers in the country, away from the danger, and remained there for the length of the war. While this helped children—and their parents—cope with the more physical dangers of the war, the emotional effects were felt years after the war ended. A drastic change to the basic family structure like this, or even a change in discipline or routines or family communication, may be the only way family members can handle their own stress. But all of these changes make you feel less secure, and make it harder for you to handle additional, future stresses.

What can you do?

In order to help prevent PTSD, even if you have suffered a traumatic experience, several things need to happen. You need to have already learned certain skills, skills that will help you withstand stress. You need to feel strong enough and confident enough to handle the trauma—and move beyond it. You need to accept reality—that bad things can happen—and yet understand that they will not always happen. You must believe that you do have some control over yourself and your world. You must lean on the people you love—the people who can offer you support and comfort. You must listen to your own voice—the internal tape recorder that reminds you of who you are, what really matters to you, and how you can make a difference in your own life and the lives of others.

These protective mechanisms may be seriously challenged by trauma. PTSD is most likely to occur if your history has already been negative, if your family, your teachers, and your friends have been mean or critical, or if they themselves are clearly afraid and unable to cope. It may occur if you are already shy, insecure, depressed, and anxious, or if your internal tape recorder is programmed with only negative messages. You will be vulnerable to the full destructive impact of trauma, and there may be symptoms of PTSD.

But there is a hopeful message in this book—a message that you can go on after a major trauma. The key is to learn how to reprocess, or re-evaluate, the

The key to moving past a traumatic event seems to be in developing successful coping strategies. By reprocessing and re-evaluating a traumatic event with the help of family, friends, or a therapist, many people with PTSD are able to reduce their fears.

events that have taken place. In Chapter 5, you will learn how therapists can help in this process.

Many trauma victims do not develop symptoms of PTSD. In some cases, it is because they manage to reprocess or re-examine the traumatic event on their own, or with the help of parents or friends, in a way that enables them to move on with their lives. Let's examine what this reprocessing can accomplish. The victim or witness needs to realistically think about what has happened and how likely it is that it would happen again. They then need to recognize and label their emotional reaction and to learn some strategies to control negative emotions such as rage, hatred, guilt

How can you re-evaluate a traumatic event to help combat PTSD?

or shame. Sometimes even repeating a comforting phrase, like "calm down . . . everything will be all right," will work.

Next, the victim must ask himself whether he is somehow feeling responsible for the event or his reaction to it. And, finally and most important, this reexamination must become part of an overall plan of responses for the future. This plan will help to change your thoughts about the event in the future, making it more bearable, reducing stress, and encouraging you to take advantage of the support of friends or family.

It's normal to think about revenge or retaliation. It's normal to worry that something terrible may happen again. But by studying the event realistically, by thinking about the likelihood that it could happen again, by studying your own emotional responses and learning to deal with them, you will find that you are focusing less often and less intensely on what happened.

Revealing

In order to cope, PTSD victims need strong relationships with their parents, siblings, and even teachers. If these relationships exist, you can receive the love, support, and help you need. Don't worry that it is somehow immature to depend on your parents, or to ask an adult for help. Don't be afraid to admit that you're afraid. Don't let the traumatic event keep you a victim forever. Lean on the people who are there to help you.

Do I have PTSD?

Colin spends most of his days feeling afraid. His friends do not know this—he plays football and hockey, and never complains about anything. They would be surprised to know that he has trouble sleeping, that his heart races every time a plane from the nearby airport flies overhead, that he worries about his family when he is away from them at school. But Colin was in New York City with his parents on September 11, 2001, the day that the World Trade Center was destroyed by terrorists. Colin and his parents had been at a museum in another part of the city and were not really close to the disaster. But they could see the smoke in the distance and, later, watched what had happened on television. Ever since then, Colin has felt frightened and uncertain. He has trouble sleeping, and can't concentrate in school. He spends his days—and nights—waiting for something terrible to happen.

If you are reading this book, you probably have more than a casual interest in PTSD. Perhaps you have some of the symptoms but not others. Perhaps you have been subjected to

Unexpected and powerful fears can be confusing. Understanding PTSD begins by identifying its symptoms. The simple questionnaire in this chapter may help you know whether you have PTSD.

violence or abuse or a bad accident and it still worries you but you are not sure whether what you are experiencing is normal or not.

You may need to see a professional to evaluate your present symptoms and history and make a determination of whether you need help. There are some things that you can do to help you better understand your current situation.

These suggestions are not a substitute for a more detailed evaluation by a mental health professional. But they may give you a rough idea as to whether or not you need to seek counseling or other medical assistance.

Rate yourself: Twenty Questions

This section provides a set of questions that you can use to examine your symptoms and gain some awareness of how serious they may be. Answer each question as honestly as possible. Your answers should indicate whether or not it is likely you have PTSD and should seek professional help.

(The questions are consistent with criteria developed by the American Psychiatric Association. However, they are presented here for illustration only, and are neither approved nor endorsed by the American Psychiatric Association in their present form. You should talk to a doctor if you think you have an anxiety disorder like PTSD.)

1. I was present at a serious event in which I or others could have been seriously injured or killed.
2. I feel really scared.
3. I can't stop thinking about the event.
4. I keep having bad dreams about the event.
5. Sometimes I seem to relive the event and it seems real.
6. Whenever I think about the event I get stomachaches or headaches or I start to sweat.
7. Whenever I think about the event I get really scared.
8. I try hard not to think about the event.
9. I stay away from things that would remind me of the event.
10. I can't seem to remember the event or some important part of it.
11. Since the event I don't want to engage in certain activities that I used to enjoy.

12. I feel detached, different, and apart from others.
13. I don't have normal feelings anymore.
14. I don't believe that I will lead a normal life.
15. I have trouble falling or staying asleep.
16. I am more irritable now and I get angry easily.
17. I have trouble concentrating.
18. I am always on my guard, expecting something bad to happen.
19. I startle easily.
20. I have trouble functioning normally at home, in school, or in other situations.

If you answered YES to most of these questions, it is likely that you are suffering from PTSD and it is important that you seek professional help. Even if you answered YES to some of the questions, and you experienced a traumatic event over a month ago, you also may be suffering enough to benefit from professional help.

Assessment

Your school counselor or family doctor can help you find a qualified mental health professional. This is what will happen: First, you will probably be given a more thorough assessment of your current psychological condition. You will be asked about your history, your family relationships, your experiences at school adjustment, and what current symptoms you may have. You will be given a more thorough evaluation of the information you have already revealed on the self-assessment. The professional—probably a licensed psychologist, psychiatrist, social worker, or counselor—will have experience in determining how serious your condition is.

Psychologists use a variety of tests to measure your emotional health. These include certain tests that ask you to answer a series of questions about the presence of certain symptoms. These tests compare your answers with those of large numbers of people with different groups of symptoms. If your answers are similar to those of persons with specific diagnoses—

What should you expect

when you go for treatment with a counselor or psychologist?

PTSD, for example—it suggests that you too may have this condition.

Another group of tests are called **projective tests**. These may feature unusual objects or pictures, such as inkblots. In the inkblot test, you are asked to examine each blot and to describe what it most looks like to you. There are no right or wrong answers. What you say may be an expression of your own personal thoughts and feelings. Someone with PTSD may describe seeing very frightening images, such as volcanoes erupting or persons being attacked by monsters, reflecting their personal fear and insecurity.

Another type of projective test shows drawings or photographs of easy-to-recognize figures doing various activities. The task is to make up a story about the picture, indicating what is happening, what people are feeling, and how it all turns out. As you may have guessed, people with PTSD may tell stories that reflect their previous trauma experiences.

Some psychologists use dolls and models and ask you to arrange the pieces to tell a story. This technique has the same general purpose as projective tests but may also be used to help you reexamine the traumatic experience as a kind of "play therapy."

The psychologist will try to interpret your test responses and come to a better understanding of what

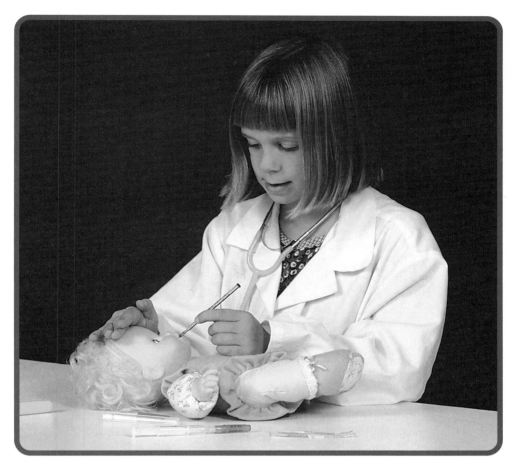

In treating people with PTSD, some therapists use dolls to help patients examine a traumatic event by playing out the experience in a safe environment.

you may be feeling. She may recommend treatment for your emotional and social problems. She may also be qualified to help you with this treatment themselves, or she may refer you to someone who is. In some cases, it may be recommended that you begin taking medication that is specifically designed to treat anxiety. If you are to receive psychotherapy or counseling, it may take various forms. Some of these are discussed in Chapter 5.

Treatment

■ Colin and his classmates gathered for a school assembly the week after the World Trade Center bombings. The principal and the school counselor spoke to the students, and told them it was normal for them to feel shocked, sad, and scared after such a tragic event. Colin was scared, but he didn't feel normal—his friends on the football team didn't look scared, and a few of them even joked about the questions some of the other kids asked the counselor. Colin still couldn't sleep well or pay attention in class, and he jumped every time someone made a noise in class. At the end of the assembly, the counselor said that anyone who wanted to talk to her could come to her office during a free period. Colin needed to talk, but he had never been to a counselor and didn't know what to expect.

Therapists and counselors are not all alike. Depending upon their training, they may treat you somewhat differently. Many approaches are effective with PTSD. However, it is

There are several different kinds of therapy—some therapists focus on behavior and symptoms, others on the way thoughts relate to feelings. Some prescribe medications, while others do not. It's important for people with PTSD to find a therapist they are comfortable with.

important that you be sure the professional you choose is licensed or certified to provide treatment and that he or she has experience in treating PTSD. It's okay to ask. Some methods found to be effective in treating PTSD are described below.

Changing the environment

As we learned in Chapter 3, there are often reminders in your surroundings that make you feel anxious. If these can be identified, and then eliminated or reduced, your anxiety and distress may be reduced until you have reached the point where you can deal better with those reminders.

Behavior therapy

Studies have revealed that PTSD can be best treated by focusing directly on its symptoms. One of these is anxiety. Approaches that teach people how to reduce anxiety are especially powerful in treating PTSD.

Behavior therapy concentrates directly upon symptoms, helping you to "un-learn" a response that was triggered (or "learned") as a way to cope with trauma. One method, called muscle relaxation, makes use of the fact that muscles become tense in various parts of the body when you feel anxious. By teaching you ways to relax your muscles, a therapist can

> **How can a therapist**
>
> **help you overcome symptoms of PTSD?**

help you reduce the feelings of anxiety. Another method, called **systematic desensitization**, uses your imagination to gradually re-introduce you to situations related to the trauma, until it no longer sparks anxious feelings.

John's story provides a useful illustration of how behavior therapy works. John was referred to a behavioral psychologist to deal with his fear of getting into cars—a fear sparked by the traumatic incident in a parking garage that we read about at the beginning of Chapter 2. The psychologist interviewed John in great detail about the traumatic incident. John was asked to describe the car, the garage, exactly where he was sitting, and what he was thinking and feeling as the car rocked dangerously over the edge. Then John was told how to relax the muscles of his body, one area at a time, until he found he could replace his anxious feelings with calm feelings, simply by controlling his muscles. The therapist then asked John to imagine himself entering the garage while trying to remain relaxed. John was asked to picture the scene as accurately as he could. He practiced this, over and over again, until he could do it without feeling anxious. Next, the therapist talked about taking the elevator to the fifth floor, where the car was located. Again, John practiced this image until he could do it comfortably. In this way, the therapist described scenes for John to imagine that were closer and closer to actually getting into the car. After several treatment sessions, John could think of himself teetering on the edge without feeling anxious. The next step required that John and his father repeat the scenes that the therapist had described—this time not in their imagination, but live. They were to do it gradually until John could handle each step without stress, before moving on to the next step. In a very short period of time, John was able to enter cars without feeling anxious.

Cognitive therapy

While behavioral techniques, such as systematic desensitization, are very useful in treating PTSD, they are often not sufficient to deal with all aspects of the emotional disorder. If you suffer from PTSD, your thoughts about the traumatic event may be closely related to the anxiety you experienced. Often these thoughts are not realistic or rational, but they seem believable to you. In Chapter 3 we discussed some of the steps that need to be taken in order to begin to deal with the trauma. These include: believing that you are no longer in danger (you must believe that you are no longer

**Some cases of PTSD can be treated with "systematic desensitization."
A victim of a car wreck, for example, might gradually conquer his fear
by systematically learning to associate calm feelings with the people,
places, and things linked to the initial accident.**

in danger in order not to feel frightened); replacing feelings of helplessness with confidence (confidence that coping is possible and that you have what it takes to do it); and relying on the support system (friends, family, counselors) available to you.

A cognitive therapist is trained to examine your thoughts and how they are related to your symptoms. This approach to therapy focuses on thoughts first, with the idea that your thoughts and beliefs determine your emotions and behavior. If it becomes clear to the therapist that your thoughts may be irrational, it is her job to challenge them and help you develop more realistic thoughts. The therapist will ask questions like, "Is there any other way you might think about this situation?" "Why do you think that will happen?" "Do you need to be thinking about this now?" This

Can you describe

the different types of therapy a counselor or psychologist may use to treat PTSD?

approach is one of the most frequently used types of psychotherapy.

But there are other effective approaches to treatment. Traditional therapy relies heavily upon talking about the incident, uncovering things that may have been forgotten, and processing this material. Other types of treatment use a combination of desensitization and cognitive therapy. A relatively new technique, called Eye Movement and Desensitization Reprocessing, seems to incorporate both techniques. In this type of therapy, the PTSD victim is taught to use eye movements similar to those that occur during dreaming. Reports indicate that this method can be effective in reducing anxiety. Yet another technique is called biofeedback. In this therapy, the functions and movements of the body (things like muscle activities) provide information, which is then processed and relayed, sometimes as a tone or signal that you can hear. These biofeedback signals can clearly tell you whether or not you are relaxed and help you begin to change your body's response to anxiety. Some therapists use hypnotherapy to treat people suffering from PTSD. Hypnosis may be helpful in situations where the patient does not recall the trauma and needs help to become aware of what happened in order to begin the healing process.

Because family support is essential for healing, many

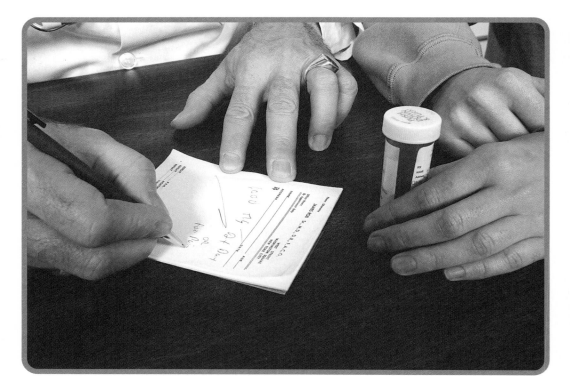

Licensed psychiatrists are medical doctors who can prescribe medications for a range of mood disorders. Using specific drugs under a doctor's care, many patients can relieve the fears associated with PTSD.

therapists find it helpful to include the family in the treatment process. Family therapy is an extremely useful strategy to make sure that the family is aware of the sufferer's feelings and understands the supportive role they must play. Family therapy explores family relationships and communication and may provide a safe place where everyone can openly discuss their feelings. Since the family may also have been involved in the trauma, even if they did not develop PTSD symptoms, it is helpful to compare everyone's thoughts about and reactions to what happened.

Finally, there some therapists who use medication to treat PTSD. Drugs that affect mental processes are called **psychotropic medications**. There are several effective medications that reduce anxiety. Some work on **neurotransmitters**—chemical messengers that conduct nerve impulses from one nerve cell to another. Others work on the sympathetic nervous system—the part of the nervous system that produces emotional reactions. (Remember that fight or flight reaction?) Your family doctor can refer you to a licensed psychiatrist who can best evaluate if you should be taking medication and can prescribe it for you.

It is clear that there are many different kinds of therapy, and many different approaches to treating PTSD. The important message is that PTSD can be treated successfully. Help is available. It is important to choose a competent and experienced therapist, one with whom you can feel comfortable.

Who's in Charge?

■ Sandy's flashbacks subsided when she talked to a therapist about being sexually abused by her father, but she was depressed and had negative thoughts. She felt like a victim, like bad things would always happen to her. A few weeks after she started therapy, Sandy started working on a history paper that was assigned to her class. She was supposed to write about someone she admired from the Revolutionary War—Sandy chose Molly Pitcher. She learned about how Molly brought water to the American soldiers during battles, and even manned a cannon when one of the Continental soldiers collapsed! Sandy admired Molly's courage in the face of danger, her desire to help other people, and her ability to overcome any obstacle in her way. Sandy wanted to develop those qualities in herself. She made a vow to work hard in therapy and never give in to her negative thoughts or to think of herself as a victim because she was abused. She knew that she could overcome her abuse, and any problem or trauma in the future. Sandy decided that she was in charge of her life.

Moving past anxious or sad feelings may seem impossible. People with PTSD must learn to develop the skills and talents within themselves to move forward without fear.

There are times when we all imagine what it would be like to have some sort of superpower, just like the superheroes in comic books. Maybe you have wondered what it would be like to be able to become invisible, or to be able to fly, or to have super-strength.

PTSD victims feel helpless—unable to prevent the trauma from continuing to haunt them, unable to protect themselves, unable to feel safe. They feel more like victims than survivors.

A superhero's strength would certainly be useful, and if another person was responsible for the trauma it is tempting to imagine how you would deal with them if only you had the necessary superpowers. But seeking revenge is not the answer. What you need cannot be found in comic books, but inside yourself. In this chapter, we will talk about how you can find, inside yourself, the skills and talents you will need to move forward.

You didn't always feel scared. You weren't born that way. You didn't always feel the need to look over your shoulder. You learned these behaviors. What is learned can be unlearned. The secret lies in gaining control of yourself. That includes your feelings, attitudes, and actions.

No one can control external events. You can plan ahead. You can anticipate bad consequences and try to avoid them. You will be successful some of the time. Some people are more cautious than others and some more successful than others at making their way around pitfalls and obstacles in life. But no one can do that perfectly. Despite your best efforts, sometimes you will be blind-sided and bad things will happen. You will forget to study something important for an exam. Accidents will happen. Someone will get hurt or even die. You may experience trauma. Such things can't always be prevented. It is how you think about those events and how you handle them emotionally that counts, more than the bad events themselves.

How would you feel if you had no control over a traumatic situation?

When trauma occurs it is an external event—it comes from outside you. Someone may have attacked you. Perhaps it was abuse coming from a family member. It might be a natural disaster or an automobile accident, or a fire . . . the possibilities are endless. There are several ways you might react to such an event. You might blame your-self. You might think that you were somehow responsible, that your actions could have controlled what happened. People sometimes have a tendency to blame the victim, which will make you feel even more guilty. Perhaps it was an accident to your younger brother. You were nearby, perhaps baby sitting. You blame yourself for not paying close enough attention.

These kinds of thoughts are destructive and unhealthy. Even if you were somehow at fault, you didn't do it on purpose. You did not intend for something terrible to happen. No one is perfect. Everyone makes mistakes. Sometimes the results are catastrophic. Negative events are complex, not black or white but shades of gray. By allowing yourself to take on all the blame for what happened, you will find yourself feeling depressed, guilty, worthless and helpless.

The trauma came from outside. It was unexpected, unpredictable, no matter how careful you were. Earthquakes, tornados, and acts of terrorism cannot be easily predicted. You are aware of that. It is natural to feel powerless and helpless. But because you were helpless in one situation does not mean you are now permanently at risk. You may conclude that you are no longer safe, perpetually in danger. It is from this kind of incorrect thinking that PTSD develops.

Research has shown that people who are optimistic—who understand that bad things can happen, and that there is little they can do to prevent them, but that they will be temporary—are healthier and more successful in life. People who are pessimistic—who feel somehow respon-sible for the bad things that happen to them, and believe that the bad things will continue to happen to them—are more depressed and feel helpless.

Many traumatic events, like natural disasters, are beyond our control. But we needn't let feelings of helplessness overwhelm us. The ideas we have about ourselves and the things that happen to us have a great influence on the way we deal with traumatic events.

Here is an example of how this kind of thinking works. Two students took the same test and both received the same grade—an F. The first student (the optimistic thinker) tells himself, "That test was unfair. The teacher asked questions that he hadn't taught and weren't covered in the book. Anyway, it was only one test. There will be several more. I will study harder for the next test and I'm sure I will ace it." The second student (the pessimistic thinker) handles the failure differently: "Oh my gosh. I failed. I'll never

> **When bad things happen**
>
> do you blame yourself, or think positively about how to correct the situation?

pass this course. I'm going to flunk out of school. I'm stupid." Which student do you think becomes depressed?

Now you are asked to take a giant step forward. Up to now, this book has focused upon the nature of PTSD and healing. These issues are important and necessary for you to go on. But they are not enough. If we were to stop here you might gain a great deal of information needed to help you cope with PTSD. If you were able to follow all the suggestions given, even psychotherapy, and treatment went well, you might achieve a satisfying degree of healing.

But you deserve more than just a quick fix for the bad things in your life. It is equally important to build positive qualities. Merely treating your symptoms of PTSD is only the beginning. You also need to reexamine your beliefs about yourself and how they influence your behavior.

The power of you

If you learn nothing else from reading this book, learn this: For many years, psychologists believed that human behavior depended on the influence of internal needs and external forces in the environment. This was an inadequate view of human nature. It failed to take into account the role of thoughts, planning, and self-direction. Behavior is a complex interaction of our thoughts and feelings, our genetic makeup, and our environment. External events don't cause our behavior. It is how we interpret those

As people with PTSD begin to understand their thoughts and feelings, they can begin to overcome their anxiety and regain control of their lives.

events, how we perceive our own behaviors and our capabilities, and how we anticipate the results of our behavior that determines how we behave, even how we feel. We can observe others and use them as models. We can evaluate our skills and capabilities. We can process these factors. We can reflect upon them. We can memorize them.

Then we can begin to change our behavior. We can change our environment. We can set goals for ourselves. We can plan ways to achieve these goals. These facts mean that humans control their own destinies. They can make things happen by their own actions. This is a general statement about how we, as humans, function. It is also a specific statement about what you can accomplish with your PTSD symptoms and with your life.

Your history may include the fact that you were abused or raped, or attacked, or injured. These events alone cannot by themselves cause you to be constantly afraid, on your guard, running away from what might happen in the future. But they can if you let them. If you believe that you are fragile, vulnerable, helpless, your dreams and hopes for yourself will be affected. Your ability to succeed at school and in relationships will be affected. You will find it harder and harder to cope. You will become anxious and depressed. The life choices you make will be affected.

But you can change how you view yourself. Positive role models, support persons, and therapists can influence you in a positive direction. You can re-evaluate your own capabilities. You can learn new skills—new strengths to enhance how you view yourself. Your positive beliefs about yourself will help you come up with realistic goals and reach them. You will be better able to manage yourself—and your emotions. This is not just pop psychology. There is solid scientific research that backs up these ideas.

> **What can you do**
>
> to change the way you see yourself?

What now?

Take a good look at yourself. Think about what you would like to accomplish. Don't worry about the obstacles. Express your hopes and dreams. Tell yourself a story—a story in which you are the hero. Think about what your character needs to accomplish to become the hero you want him or her to be. We're talking about more than getting rid of negatives here. Choose qualities that others will value. Choose them not because your parents or your teachers or your minister says so (although these are valuable inputs), but because that is what you want and what you are capable of achieving. Go for it.

Glossary

Anxiety disorder — a condition, such a PTSD, in which feelings of anxiety are persistent, unprovoked, and out-of-control.

Behavior therapy — therapy that concentrates on symptoms and is designed to help the patient "unlearn" responses triggered by situations similar to a past trauma.

Defenses — behaviors that help reduce anxiety.

Dissociative state — a mental state in which the sufferer is disconnected from and not fully aware of self, time, and/or external circumstances.

Fight or flight mechanism — a biological response to an emergency that prepares the body to fight a predator or flee a dangerous situation.

Flashbacks — a vivid reliving of a past traumatic experience that appears real to the individual experiencing it.

Neurotransmitters — chemical messengers that conduct nerve impulses from one nerve cell to another.

Phobias — an exaggerated and inexplicable fear of a particular object or situation.

Post-traumatic stress disorder (PTSD) — an anxiety disorder that causes the sufferer to relive a trauma, to avoid situations similar to that trauma, and to be anxious and expectant of future traumatic events.

Projective tests — therapeutic tools, such as ink blot tests, patients are asked to interpret as a means of revealing thoughts and feelings.

Psychotropic medications — drugs that affect mental processes.

Stressors — influences or factors that may cause anxiety.

Glossary

Survival mechanisms — physical skills and responses that help an animal, including human beings, survive in an emergency or dangerous situation.

Systematic desensitization — a technique used by a therapist to retrain a patient to approach frightening situations without anxiety.

Trauma — a disordered psychological or behavioral state resulting from mental or emotional stress, or physical injury.

Further Reading

Bandura, A. *Self-efficacy: The Exercise of control.* New York: Freeman, 1997.

Beck, A. T., Rush, A. J., Shaw, B. F., Emery, G. *Cognitive Therapy of Depression.* New York: Guilford Press, 1979.

Ellis, A. *Humanistic Psychology: The Rational Emotive Approach.* New York: McGraw-Hill, 1973.

Huber, C. *There's Nothing Wrong With You for Teens.* Murphys, CA: Keep it Simple Books, 2001.

Maslow, A. H. *Toward a Psychology of Being.* New York: Von Nostrand , Reinhold, 1954.

McGraw, J. *Life Strategies for Teens.* New York: Simon & Schuster, 2000.

Rogers, C. R. *On Becoming a Person.* Boston: Houghton Mifflin, 1961.

Seligman, M. E. P. *Learned Optimism.* New York: A. A. Knopf, 1991.

Index

Index

About the Author

Marvin Rosen is a licensed clinical psychologist who practices in Media, Pennsylvania. He received his doctorate degree from the University of Pennsylvania in 1961. Since 1963, he has worked with intellectually and emotionally challenged people at Elwyn, Inc. in Pennsylvania, with clinical, administrative, research, and training responsibilities. He also conducts a private practice of psychology. Dr. Rosen has taught psychology at the University of Pennsylvania, Bryn Mawr College, and West Chester University. He has written or edited seven book and numerous professional articles in the areas of psychology, rehabilitation, emotional disturbance, and mental retardation.